Animals

Penny King & Clare Roundhill

A & C Black · London

Designed by Jane Warring

Illustrations by Lindy Norton

Children's pictures by
Amber Civardi, Camilla Cramsie, Louise Cramsie, Charlotte
Downham, Lara Haworth, Lucinda Howells, Sophie Johns,
Lucy MacDonald Watson, Zoë More O'Ferrall,
Gussie Pownhall, Thomas Stofer, Ned Wyndham
Pottery by Chloë Thomson

Picture research by Sara Elliott

Photographs by Peter Millard

Reprinted 1999, 2002
First paperback edition 1996
First published 1996 in hardback by
A & C Black Publishers Ltd
37 Soho Square, London, W1D 3QZ
www.acblack.com

Created by
Thumbprint Books

Copyright © 1996 Thumbprint Books

A CIP catalogue record for this book is available from the British Library

ISBN 0-7136-6701-X

Printed and bound in Singapore

A & C Black uses paper produced with elemental chlorine-free pulp,
harvested from managed, sustainable forests.

Cover photograph: Franz Marc Blue Horse 1 1911
Franz Marc was a German artist who particularly loved nature and animals. He thought animals
were more beautiful and purer than people. He tried to give the animals life by painting them in
vivid, strong colours and showing flowing movements.

Contents

Animals in art

Animals have been shown in art throughout history, ever since prehistoric man first painted them on cave walls. They have been admired, loved and feared for their speed, strength, cunning, fierceness or skill.

Muséum d' Histoire Naturelle, Le Havre

Sometimes animals were worshipped as gods or used as symbols of power or good luck. In Ancient Egypt, the cat was thought to be a goddess who guarded people against diseases and evil spirits. At other times, animals were painted or sculpted because of their beauty or because they were much-loved pets.

Before photography, explorers took artists with them on their expeditions so that they could paint the animals they found. These paintings were often realistic and gave people who had never seen a wild animal an idea of how it looked.

Pictures are also a useful way of finding out about all kinds of animals that are now extinct. Cave paintings show what a mammoth looked like. On one expedition, an artist painted a picture, like this, to show what a dodo looked like.

In this book, there are six animal works of art. Each of them has been created for a different purpose and uses a different technique.

You can learn what gave the artists their ideas and discover how they made the pictures and sculptures. Borrow their ideas, mix them with your own and create stunning animal works of art. The pictures done by children will also help you.

Start by painting your own pet or a friend's pet, or copy an animal from a magazine or a photograph. Zoo and wildlife parks are good places to find rarer animals to paint.

You may want to paint realistic pictures with lots of detail, or just sketch an animal in its surroundings. Think about its colouring or the pattern of its coat. Is it furry or smooth? Does it have big or small ears? What shape is its tail?

Prehistoric paintings

Deep in a cave at Lascaux, in France,
are wonderful wall paintings of cows,
horses, bison, stags and even a woolly
rhinoceros. They were painted thousands
of years ago, but no one knows exactly
why. Some people think that the
cave was a place of worship.

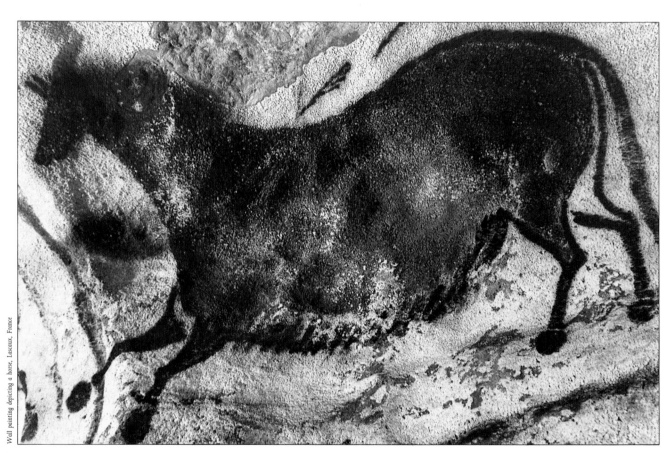

Wall painting depicting a horse, Lascaux, France

Three French boys discovered the
paintings over fifty years ago, quite
by accident. They were out for a
walk when their dog disappeared
down a hole in a hillside. One of
the boys went to search for him.

The ground beneath the boy gave
way and he tumbled into a cave,
followed by his friends. They lit
matches to see where they were,
and were amazed to find hundreds
of animals painted on the walls.

The prehistoric artists had used soil and rocks to make red, black, yellow and white colours. They mixed them with sand or clay, crushed them with stones into powder and added water from the cave.

They painted with their fingers or used brushes made of animal hair or twigs with chewed ends. They worked by the flickering light of tallow (animal fat) lamps.

The artists were very skilled. They never changed or rubbed out any of their marks. They used bumps and cracks in the walls to bring out the shapes of the animals.

Their paintings are full of realistic details about the animals. Ibex (a kind of goat) are shown fighting and bison are shown shedding their winter coats. Some of the horses have detailed markings on their coats.

Stone Age pictures

Imagine you are an artist living in the Stone Age. There are no shops for you to buy paints or paintbrushes. You are going to have to make them yourself.

You may not be able to grind up rocks to make colours like prehistoric people did, but there are all sorts of things that you can use to make your own natural colours, such as plants, fruits, earth and vegetables. It's easy to make your own brushes, too, or you can just paint with your fingers.

Prehistoric paintbrushes

Make paintbrushes with bundles of dried grass tied together, or with feathers. You could also use a twig. Flatten one end with a stone first.

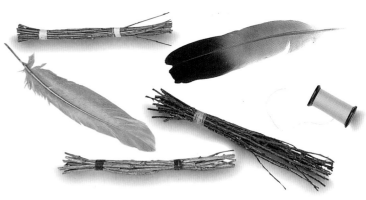

Mixing natural colours

Squash raspberries, strawberries or blackberries through a sieve to make rich reds. Ask an adult to boil some onion skins in a little water to make orange, and some green leaves or grass to make green. Red cabbage and beetroot both give a good purple. Wait until the water has cooled before you use it.

Soil mixed with a little water will make brown. Ground chalk and water will make white.

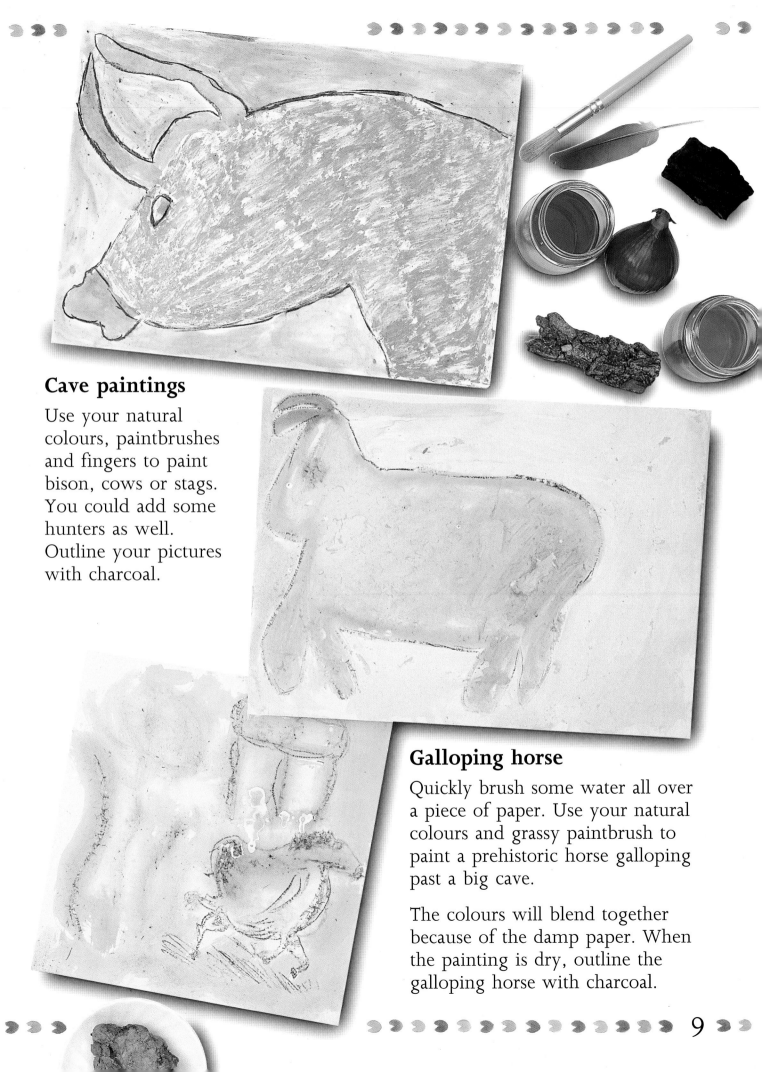

Cave paintings

Use your natural colours, paintbrushes and fingers to paint bison, cows or stags. You could add some hunters as well. Outline your pictures with charcoal.

Galloping horse

Quickly brush some water all over a piece of paper. Use your natural colours and grassy paintbrush to paint a prehistoric horse galloping past a big cave.

The colours will blend together because of the damp paper. When the painting is dry, outline the galloping horse with charcoal.

A two-headed snake

This wriggly two-headed snake was made by an Aztec craftsman in Mexico, about 500 years ago. It is made of wood covered with pieces of precious blue turquoise stone. The mouths and noses are made of red coral and the teeth are made of shell.

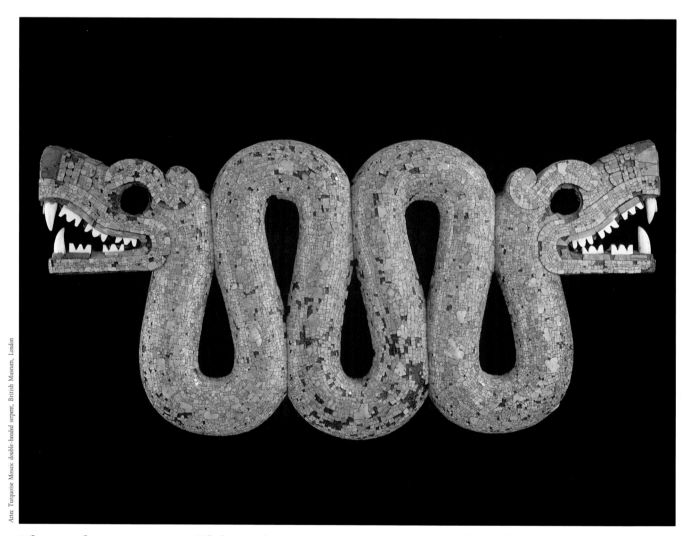

Aztec Turquoise Mosaic double-headed serpent, British Museum, London

The snake represents Tlaloc, the Aztec rain god. The two heads show the coming and going of rain. The Aztecs believed that it was Tlaloc who watered their crops and made them grow.

The Aztecs thought they would starve if they did not keep Tlaloc happy. To pray for rain, they held many festivals throughout the year, where they danced, feasted and sacrificed people.

The Aztecs believed that different gods looked after every part of their lives. These gods gave them sun, fire, wind, learning, and greatness.

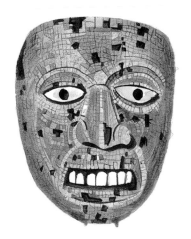

◀ Quetzalcoatl (the plumed serpent) was the god of creation, learning and holiness. This mask of him is made from wood covered with pieces of turquoise.

▶ Huitzilopochtli was the sun god.

◀ Xiuhtectihtli was the god of fire.

▶ Aztec nobles measured their wealth and power by the richness of the things that they owned, and the clothes that they wore.

Skilled craftsmen made beautiful things to wear in gold, silver and precious stones. These pieces, such as the snake, the mask and jewellery, were worn only on special ceremonial days.

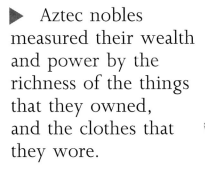

11

Scaly reptiles

You can make your own precious snake fit for a king or queen. The best materials to use are self-hardening clay and brightly coloured oven-baked modelling clay which you can buy in craft shops. Before you start to mould it, soften it in your hands.

Ask an adult to help you bake it in the oven to harden it. The directions are usually written on the packet.

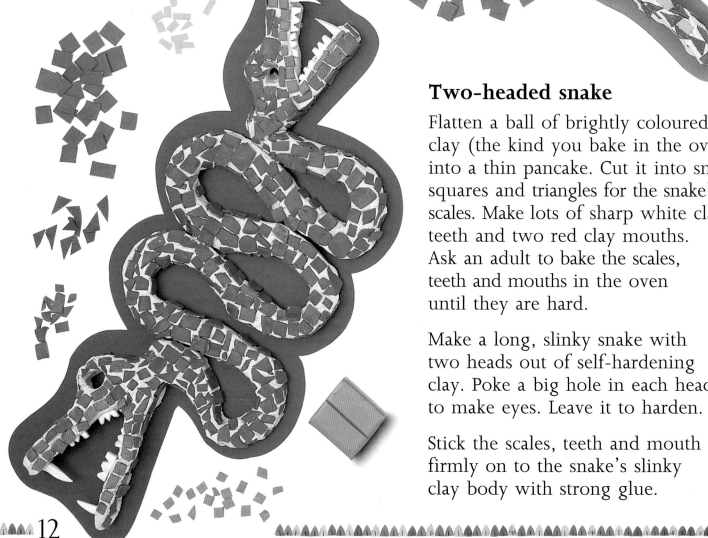

Two-headed snake

Flatten a ball of brightly coloured clay (the kind you bake in the oven) into a thin pancake. Cut it into small squares and triangles for the snake's scales. Make lots of sharp white clay teeth and two red clay mouths. Ask an adult to bake the scales, teeth and mouths in the oven until they are hard.

Make a long, slinky snake with two heads out of self-hardening clay. Poke a big hole in each head to make eyes. Leave it to harden.

Stick the scales, teeth and mouth firmly on to the snake's slinky clay body with strong glue.

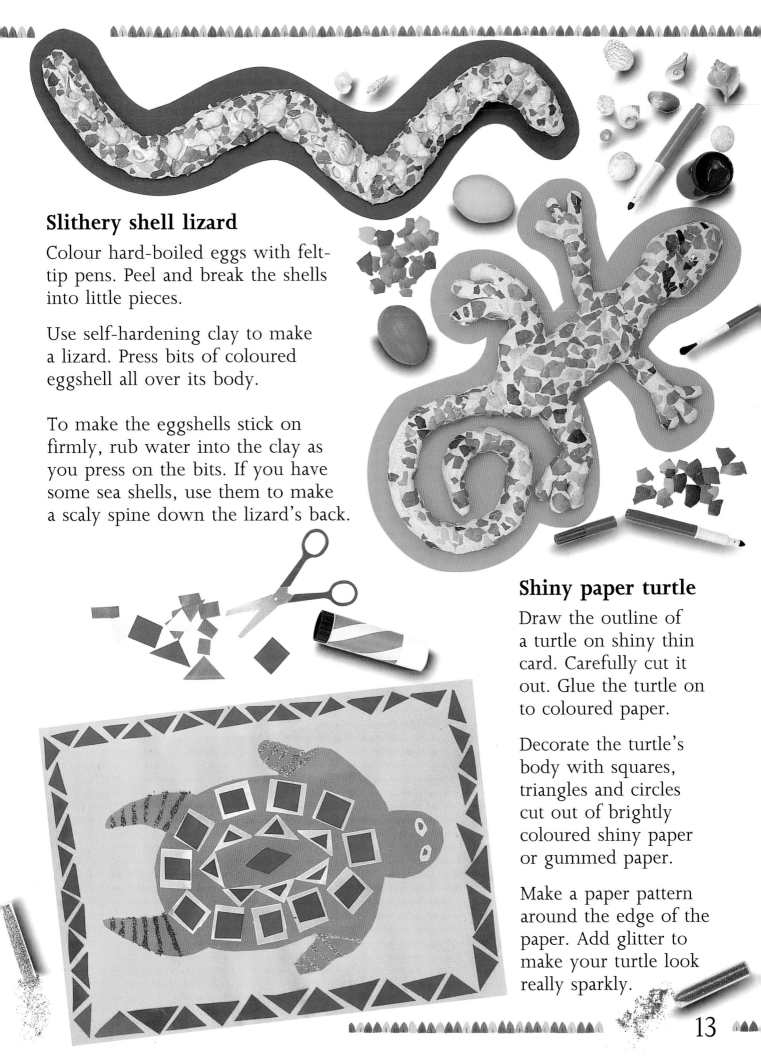

Slithery shell lizard

Colour hard-boiled eggs with felt-tip pens. Peel and break the shells into little pieces.

Use self-hardening clay to make a lizard. Press bits of coloured eggshell all over its body.

To make the eggshells stick on firmly, rub water into the clay as you press on the bits. If you have some sea shells, use them to make a scaly spine down the lizard's back.

Shiny paper turtle

Draw the outline of a turtle on shiny thin card. Carefully cut it out. Glue the turtle on to coloured paper.

Decorate the turtle's body with squares, triangles and circles cut out of brightly coloured shiny paper or gummed paper.

Make a paper pattern around the edge of the paper. Add glitter to make your turtle look really sparkly.

Tropical tiger

How would you like to come face to face with a crouching tiger in the middle of a wild and windy storm? Henri Rousseau, the French artist who painted this picture, became famous for exotic jungle scenes like this.

Henri Rousseau *Surprise!* 1891, The National Gallery, London

In some of his jungle pictures, fierce lions and tigers are shown attacking their prey. Others show mischievous monkeys playing, or mysterious people. Rousseau boasted that he got the ideas for these paintings from travelling to faraway places.

In fact, Rousseau never left France. He drew the tropical plants at the Botanical Gardens in Paris and copied the tiger from a children's book or from a model. The tiger's eyes look very glassy, just like those of a stuffed animal.

Rousseau did not have any training as a painter. He taught himself to draw and paint by copying famous pictures in the Louvre, a big museum in Paris.

Some people made fun of Rousseau's paintings. They thought his work was too child-like. But Picasso and several other famous artists thought he was a great artist and they once gave a banquet in his honour.

Rousseau's style of painting is very distinctive. He used clear outlines and bold colours. Everything in his pictures is very carefully painted - for example, you can see each blade of grass and every leaf on the trees.

Some of Rousseau's pictures are scenes of everyday life. But his most famous pictures are those with people or animals set in extraordinary or dream-like settings. This one is called 'The Sleeping Gypsy'.

In the jungle

If Henri Rousseau could paint a tiger in a jungle without having seen a tiger or visited a jungle, so could you. You could sketch a tiger from a picture in a book, or go and look at one in a zoo.

Try to make your jungle as exciting and wild as Rousseau did. Paint a dark, stormy sky, long, thick grass and tall trees bending in the strong wind.

Painted tiger

Before you start to paint your picture, mix poster paints with PVA glue and a little flour. They will then become thick and shiny, like oil paints.

Starting at the top of the paper, as Rousseau did, paint a stormy sky. Then mix yellow and blue together to make green for the trees and grass. If you want a dark green, add a little more blue. Add more yellow to make a light green.

When the paint is dry, add a fierce tiger leaping through the grass. You may need to add a few extra blades of grass to hide him.

Wax resist leopard

With wax crayons, draw a leopard in the middle of a sheet of paper. Colour in the black spots on the leopard's body, the black parts of his eyes and his white teeth.

Use more crayons to draw green leaves, bushes and trees all around him. Make them all bend the same way so that it looks windy. Draw the rain with a white crayon and the lightning with a yellow crayon.

Mix a stormy grey colour with white and a little black paint. Add a lot of water and paint the sky. Cover the leopard with thin yellow paint and the jungle with thin green paint. All the parts you drew with wax crayon will shine through the paint.

Torn tissue zebra

Make this sheltering zebra with torn strips of tissue paper and scrunched-up tissue balls.

Draw the outline of a zebra on white paper. Tear black tissue paper into thin strips. Glue these on to the zebra's body. Cut out the zebra and glue it on to green paper.

Make a tree trunk with brown tissue balls. Tear green tissue paper into leaf and grass shapes. Glue the bottom part of each leaf on to the tree. Leave the top part fluttering in the breeze. Overlap the grass strips to make them look more real.

Saint Francis and the birds

Saint Francis was an Italian saint.
He loved animals and once gave a sermon
to a flock of birds. Stanley Spencer, a
modern artist, painted a picture of this
story. He set it in Cookham, the
English village where he lived.

Stanley Spencer *Saint Francis and the Birds* 1935, Tate Gallery, London

Spencer painted Saint Francis extra
large, with outstretched arms, to show
that his teaching spread far and wide.
He is looking upwards, as if he were
talking to God. Notice how the
farmyard birds overlap, to show they
are sheltering behind Saint Francis.

This picture was entered for an
important exhibition. It was turned
down because people thought it was
too odd. Their reason was that they
thought Spencer had made a mistake
in it. Can you see what they thought
this was? (The answer is on page 32).

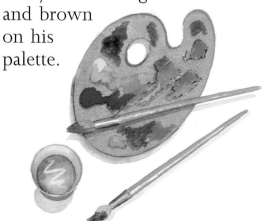

Spencer painted many pictures of Bible stories and saints. He modelled the people on his family and local villagers. He remembered how his father went outside in his dressing gown to fetch food for their hens and geese. The dressing gown reminded him of the long clothes that monks wear. This gave Spencer the idea for his picture.

The colours in the picture are earthy and natural. Spencer used them to show the link between Saint Francis and nature. He created many shades of green and brown on his palette.

Compare Spencer's picture of Saint Francis with this wall painting by Giotto, an Italian who lived 700 years ago. It is in the church at Assisi, the village where Saint Francis was born. Giotto was one of the first painters to make people look realistic. When it was first created, this painting would have seemed very modern and unusual.

Farmyard flocks

These paintings will give you ideas on how to mix colours together to get all sorts of different shades. They also show you simple ways of creating a crowd of any sort of animal.

Perhaps you'd like to paint a picture of Saint Francis and the birds. You could use one of your parents as a model and your house or village as the background.

Multicoloured duck

On a sheet of white paper, draw a simple duck with rows of feathers. Choose two primary colours that go together well - say blue and red, red and yellow or yellow and blue.

Put one colour into a pot, say yellow, and paint the first feather this colour. Add a tiny blob of the second colour, say blue. Mix it up and paint the second feather this colour. Mix a little more of the second colour to the pot and paint the third feather this colour.

Carry on doing this, remembering to add only a tiny blob of the second colour to the pot, until you have painted every feather in a different colour.

A goosey crowd

Draw a nice fat goose on a piece of thin card and then cut it out. Draw around this shape (which is called a template) on to sheets of different coloured paper. Cut out the coloured geese.

Stick the paper geese on to a piece of black paper so that they overlap one another.

Look at your picture very carefully and make a sketch of it. You could also practise drawing crowds of people or animals in the same way.

Saint Mummy or Saint Daddy

For this picture ask your mum or dad to pose for you in their dressing gown, pretending to be a saint feeding a pet.

Paint a picture of one of them while he or she is in this pose. Use lots of shades of the same colour, just as Stanley Spencer did.

21

Fante flags

The Fante people of Ghana, in West Africa, have been making these brightly coloured patchwork flags for over six hundred years. The flags are paraded through the streets of towns and villages at festivals, and at the funerals of important people.

© Asafo flag, Fish Grow Fat for the Benefit of the Crocodile, Peter Adler, London

Fante flags are made of cotton, silk, satin or felt. There can be as many as 15 different colours on one flag. Sometimes they are embroidered to give them an even more interesting texture and look.

The pictures sewn on the flags tell stories of historical events or African proverbs. They show details of the way the Fante live and their beliefs. This flag's proverb says, 'Fish grow fat for the benefit of the crocodile'.

Long ago, Fante warriors, known as Asafo, formed different groups, called companies. Each company used their own colours and designs for their flags which nobody else was allowed to copy.

The flag designs often include animals, birds, insects, reptiles and fish, some of which represent power and glory. Elephants, bush cows and whales symbolize strength. Leopards, eagles and crocodiles are admired for their hunting skills.

The proverb shown on the flag below says, 'Even if you are an able hunter never dare hunt under the tree of an eagle'.

The biggest Asafo festival is the Akwambo, which means 'path clearing'. It is about friendship and families. The flags are carried in a procession through the town, put on flagpoles or draped across houses.

Animal flags

Use squares and rectangles of felt or fabric to make your own flags. They would make good decorations for your bedroom or for a party.

If you want to make collage flags, you will need glue that sticks fabric. If you prefer to make appliqué ones, you will need a needle and thread.

Butterfly flag

Cut out a flag from a large piece of felt and glue a felt border all around it in a contrasting colour. Cut out a big, beautiful felt butterfly with two colourful wings. Carefully glue them on to the flag. Add two feelers to the top of the butterfly's head. Decorate the wings with patterns cut out of scraps of brightly coloured felt.

Appliqué animals

Draw a large animal - such as a tiger, leopard, dinosaur or monster - on a piece of felt. Cut it out. Sew on felt stripes or spots and a beady eye. Sew the animal on to a big felt flag, using running stitch. You could also sew on some trees or leaves for your animals to munch.

Pretty patterns

Cut out a big felt fish. Sew zig-zag patterns all over it, using a brightly coloured thread for each row. Sew an oval shape for the eye. Stitch the fish on to your flag. You could make a scaly crocodile, a feathery bird or a spiny porcupine in a similar way.

Aboriginal art

The Aborigines are a people who have lived in Australia for over fifty thousand years. They have carved and painted pictures on rocks, bark, wood and stone. These are often decorated with elaborate patterns. Susan Wanji Wanji is a modern Aboriginal artist, who was taught to paint when she was a little girl.

When she painted this buffalo, Susan Wanji Wanji combined old Aboriginal ideas with modern materials. Instead of making her own paints, as the Aborigines used to, she uses a modern paint called gouache.

Susan gets many of the ideas for her designs from the painted body decorations, called Tiwi jilamara, of the Aboriginal Tiwi tribe. They paint their bodies with patterns for important ceremonies.

The Aborigines have their own ideas about how the world began. They believe that everything in the world was made long ago, in a time called the 'Dreamtime'. Many of their works of art tell stories about the 'Dreamtime'.

The Aborigines decorated and painted caves and rock faces with pictures of animals, birds, fish and reptiles. They believed that if they painted these animals, they would always be able to hunt them for food.

Turtles played an important part in their lives: in stories, in dreams and as food. Look at this old turtle rock painting compared with Susan Wanji Wanji's bright and colourful modern painting.

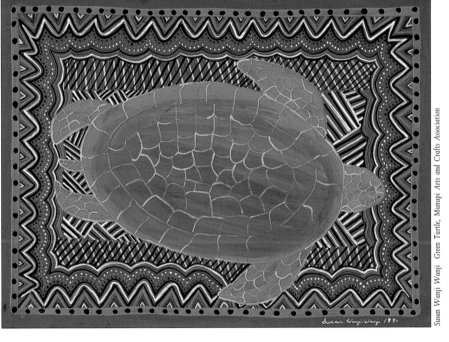

Susan Wanji-Wanji 1991

Susan Wanji Wanji Green Turtle, Munupi Arts and Crafts Association

Today, a few artists still paint on bark. First it must be dried and flattened. Then the artist covers the bark with red or yellow colour, called ochre, and draws the animal designs and delicate patterns in white pigment.

Perfect patterns

Kangaroos, wallabies, koalas and birds, such as budgerigars and cockatoos, all live in Australia. Choose the ones you would like to paint or draw and then create your own exciting Aboriginal pictures.

You can use felt-tip pens, wax crayons or fluorescent paints to cover your pictures with decorations. The brighter and the busier they are, the better.

Crazy kangaroo

Draw the outline of a kangaroo in the middle of a square piece of paper. Use a ruler to divide the background into stripes, and the kangaroo into different shapes.

Use felt-tip pens to decorate each shape on the kangaroo with a different pattern, and each of the background stripes. If you run out of ideas, look back at some of the colourful and exciting patterns Susan Wanji Wanji has used.

Wax scratch animals

Cover a piece of paper with bands of colour, using fat wax crayons. Press hard so that the colours are nice and bright. Now choose a dark wax crayon and cover the whole piece of paper with a thick layer so that the bands of colour don't show through.

Use something sharp, such as a knitting needle, to scratch a thick outline of a koala or a budgie. Scratch exciting patterns all over the animal and the background.

Perching parrot

For this picture, you will need some black paper or card and some bright fluorescent paints.

Use white to paint the outline of a big parrot in the middle of the black paper. Decorate either the bird or the background with bright patterns using different coloured fluorescent paints. If you leave the background plain, paint a patterned border around the edge of the paper.

More about the artists

Prehistoric cave painters
(c.17,000 BC   Lascaux, France)
Lascaux Horse

The cave paintings found across south-west France and northern Spain are mostly of animals. Sometimes, the artists painted hunters chasing the animals, or made handprints. The paintings are usually deep inside dark caves where humans would never have lived. This is the reason why people think they may have been painted for either magical or religious reasons.

Aztec craftsmen
(1400 - 1520   Mexico)

Turquoise Mosaic double-headed serpent
Everyone in Aztec society had a particular place. The ruler was at the top, followed by the nobles, who were governors, judges and generals. The most skilled craftsmen came just below the nobles. They lived and worked in their own area within the cities and produced precious objects which only the ruler and nobles were allowed to own. Their skills were handed down from father to son, often taking years to learn.

Henri Rousseau
(1844 - 1910   French)
Surprise! 1891

Rousseau started his career in the army and then worked at a Paris toll station (which is why he was later nicknamed 'Le Douanier', French for customs officer). When he retired, he taught himself to paint and started showing his pictures at exhibitions. Several modern artists were inspired by his simple and imaginative way of painting. Picasso, a famous twentieth-century artist, called Rousseau 'the godfather of modern painting'.

Sir Stanley Spencer
(1891 - 1959   English)
Saint Francis and the Birds 1935

Spencer lived for most of his life in Cookham, the village where he was born. He thought that Cookham was an 'earthly paradise'. His early paintings were based on people and places in the village, but they all illustrate religious stories. After the First World War, Spencer spent many years painting a War memorial chapel. The pictures in it show everyday activities in the war hospital where he worked, and soldiers washing and eating rather than fighting. During the Second World War, Spencer was made an official war artist.

Fante flagmakers
'Fish Grow Fat for the Benefit of the Crocodile (who rules the river)'

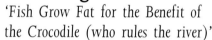

Today, a new flag is made when a new captain takes over a company. The captain pays for the flag, but it then belongs to the company. He has a say in its design, which is usually of either an animal, a famous company event or a proverb which shows the company's strength. A flagmaker then designs the pictures in his own style. New flags have to be approved by the chief of all the companies, as well as by the other local companies.

Susan Wanji Wanji
(Born 1955   Australian Aboriginal)
Buffalo 1993

Susan Wanji Wanji lives in an Aboriginal community on Melville Island in the far north of Australia, where she paints and weaves baskets in an art centre. She spends some of her time hunting, gathering and fishing, which inspires many of the ideas for her paintings.

Other things to do

1 Turn the first letter of your name into a picture of any animal you like, or into an animal that begins with the same letter as your name. If you are feeling very ambitious, you might like to turn your whole name into a zoo of animals!

3 Model some animals in clay or salt dough. This will help you think about their shapes. Make the body first and then add a head, legs, ears and a tail. Remember to score lines across and dampen the parts you are joining together. Press them firmly in place. Paint your models and varnish them when they are dry.

2 Keep a scrapbook about animals. Divide it into three parts - animals you have seen in real life; animals you have seen in books or on TV; extinct and imaginary animals, such as dodos, dinosaurs and unicorns. Practise drawing animals of your own to put in the scrapbook, as well as sticking in photographs, postcards, cartoons and any other pictures you can find.

4 Make a passport for your pet or your favourite animal. Design a grand cover for it and write the animal's name on the front. Draw a realistic picture of your animal or stick in a photograph. Describe the animal's habits, its favourite foods and funny antics. Draw sketches of it in different moods and postures.

Index

Answer to question on page 18: The hands of both Saint Francis and the boy are the wrong way round. Look at their thumbs!

Acknowledgements

The publishers are grateful to the following institutes and individuals for permission to reproduce the illustrations on the pages mentioned.
Städtische Galerie in Lenbachhaus, Munich / Artothek: cover; Muséum d'Historie Naturelle, Le Havre, (no. 80057): 4; The Ancient Art and Architecture Collection: 6; © The British Museum, London: 10; Reproduced by courtesy of the Trustees, The National Gallery, London: 14; Tate Gallery, London / © Estate of Stanley Spencer 1996 All Rights Reserved DACS: 18; San Francesco, Assisi / The Bridgeman Art Library, London: 19; © Peter Adler from Asafo! African flags of the Fante by Peter Adler and Nicholas Barnard, published by Thames and Hudson, 1992: 22 and 23; Munupi Arts and Crafts Association, Pularumpi, Melville Island, Australia © Susan Wanji Wanji: 26 and 27.